202544

GRAPHIC BIOGRAPHIES

NELSON MANDELA

THE LIFE OF AN AFRICAN STATESMAN

by
ROB SHONE

illustrated by
NEIL REED

rosen
central™

The Rosen Publishing Group, Inc., New York

Published in 2007 by The Rosen Publishing Group, Inc.
29 East 21st Street, New York, NY 10010

First edition, 2007

Designed and produced by
David West Books

Editor: Dominique Crowley
Photo Research: Victoria Cook

Photo credits:
Page 4, Library of Congress; page 5, British Pathe/ITN (both); page 6, British Pathe/ITN (all); page 7, istockphoto.com; page 44 (left), istockphoto.com; page 44/45, British Pathe/ITN; page 46, British Pathe/ITN (both)

Library of Congress Cataloging-in-Publication Data

Shone, Rob.
Nelson Mandela: the life of an African statesman / Rob Shone; illustrated by Neil Reed—1st ed.
p. cm. — (Graphic biographies)
Includes index.
ISBN 10: 1-4042-0860-7 (library binding)
ISBN 13: 978-1-4042-0860-5 (library binding)
ISBN 10: 1-4042-0923-9 (pbk.)
ISBN 13: 978-1-4042-0923-7 (pbk.)
6-Pack ISBN 10: 1-4042-0922-0
6-Pack ISBN 13: 978-1-4042-0922-0

1. Mandela, Nelson, 1918—Juvenile literature. 2. Presidents—South Africa—Biography—Juvenile literature. I. Title. II. Series: Graphic biographies (Rosen Publishing Group)

DT1974.S47 2006
968.06'5092--dc22

2005036241

Manufactured in China

CONTENTS

WHO'S WHO

Nelson Mandela (1918–) Nelson Mandela spent 27 years in prison for his opposition to the South African regime. He was released in 1990. In 1994 he became South Africa's first black president.

Winnie Mandela (1936–) Winnie, a social worker, was Nelson Mandela's second wife. She supported him throughout his long imprisonment.

F. W. de Klerk (1936–) In 1984, F. W. de Klerk succeeded P. W. Botha as South Africa's president. During his presidency, racial division was abolished and free elections were first held.

Walter Sisulu (1912–2003) Walter Sisulu was a lifelong friend of Nelson Mandela. He was sent to Robben Island with Mandela after the Rivonia Trial.

Oliver Tambo (1917–1993) Oliver Tambo first met Nelson Mandela at boarding school. He spent 30 years in exile, first as the African National Congress's representative abroad and later as its president.

P. W. Botha (1916–) P. W. Botha was South Africa's prime minister from 1978 until 1984. He was the first person to become the country's president.

SOUTH AFRICA'S PAST

When white people first arrived in Africa, they made a strong impression on the African Zulu tribe. A Zulu poet wrote, "They carry a long stick of fire. With this they loot and kill." The Zulus themselves, however, were once new to South Africa, too.

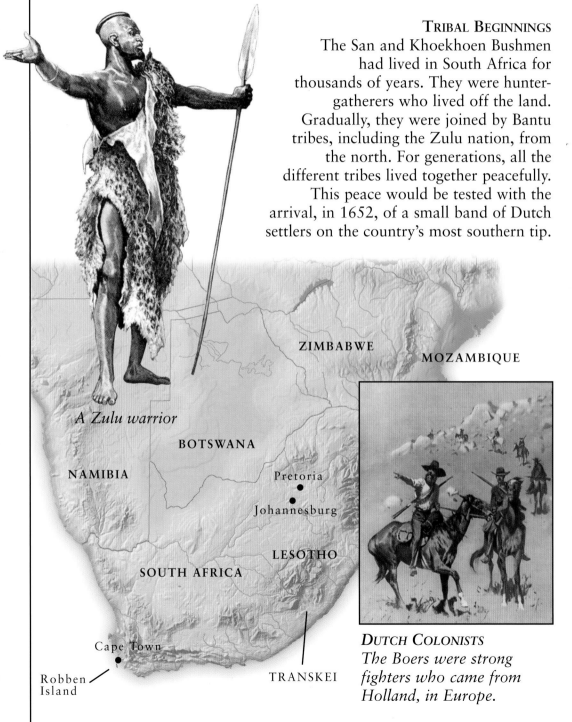

TRIBAL BEGINNINGS

The San and Khoekhoen Bushmen had lived in South Africa for thousands of years. They were hunter-gatherers who lived off the land. Gradually, they were joined by Bantu tribes, including the Zulu nation, from the north. For generations, all the different tribes lived together peacefully. This peace would be tested with the arrival, in 1652, of a small band of Dutch settlers on the country's most southern tip.

A Zulu warrior

ZIMBABWE

MOZAMBIQUE

BOTSWANA

NAMIBIA

Pretoria

Johannesburg

LESOTHO

SOUTH AFRICA

Cape Town

Robben Island

TRANSKEI

DUTCH COLONISTS
The Boers were strong fighters who came from Holland, in Europe.

THE COMING OF THE EUROPEANS

The first Dutch settlement, Cape Town, was a useful port for European trading ships sailing to the Far East. By 1814, the port and surrounding lands were under British rule. At first, the Europeans had no interest beyond the cape. This changed in 1836. The Dutch Boers, unhappy with British rule, left the cape on what became known as the Great Trek. They moved into the unexplored north and northeast areas of the country and set up their own states. The British became more interested in the South African interior when gold and diamonds were discovered there.

THE BOER WARS

The discovery of gold and diamonds led to war between the Dutch Boers and the British. In 1902, after three years of hard fighting, the Boers were defeated, and the British took control of South Africa.

INDEPENDENCE

In 1910, the British and Boer regions joined to become the Union of South Africa. Although it was part of the British Empire, it was allowed to govern itself. The first governments were formed by a pro-British group called the Union Party. In 1948, the Afrikaner National Party came to power. It represented the Boers and introduced a policy of racial division.

THE BOER WAR
The British Light Cavalry formed part of the 500,000-soldier British army that fought in the Boer War.

THE NATIONAL PARTY
Dr. Daniel Malan was the leader of South Africa's National Party.

RACIAL DIVISION

*R*acism in South Africa did not begin with the election of the National Party. Almost as soon as white settlers arrived in South Africa, the local population was discriminated against. The National Party wanted to keep white people separate from other South Africans. Most of the country's land, and all of its wealth, would be under white control.

VERWOERD
Hendrik F. Verwoerd was South Africa's prime minister from 1958 until 1966. He created the apartheid system.

THE PASS LAWS

The Pass Laws, strengthened by the Nationalists, stated that people who were not white Europeans had to carry identification at all times. They were not allowed to travel between different areas without a pass. Even with a pass, nonwhites needed permission to leave their rural areas and enter urban ones. People often protested by burning their pass books.

ROBBEN ISLAND PRISON
Nelson Mandela spent eighteen years in the prison on Robben Island.

UITSLUITLIK VIR BLANKES
EXCLUSIVELY FOR WHITES
·WINE BUFFET WYNBUFFET·

WHITES ONLY
Signs like this one, in English and the Afrikaans language, were common in South Africa.

THE GROUP AREA ACT

The Group Area Act was a rule that created different residential zones for different races. White people lived in one area, blacks in another. People who were living in the "wrong" area were arrested and forced to move out of their homes. The law also stated that the different areas did not have to be equal; often, the "white" areas were more comfortable than those for black people.

THE BANTU STATES

The Bantu States were small pockets of land set aside throughout South Africa as homelands for the various African tribes. Each tribe was ordered by the government to govern itself. Separating the tribes was intended to build traditional tribal rivalries. It also prevented them from uniting against the government. This increased the government's power.

SHANTY TOWNS

Many South Africans were forced to leave their homes due to apartheid. They had to live in slums like this one.

OPPOSITION PARTIES

*Nelson Mandela belonged to the **African National Congress (ANC)**. It believed in the unity of all South Africans.*

Pan African Congress (PAC) *This was the ANC's rival. It believed only Africans should fight racism.*

South African Indian Congress (SAIC) *The SAIC supported Indian people.*

South African Communist Party (SACP) *This party supported ordinary, working South Africans.*

Black Consciousness Movement (BCM) *The BCM called all black people to come together.*

NELSON MANDELA
THE LIFE OF AN AFRICAN STATESMAN

NINE-YEAR-OLD NELSON MANDELA AND HIS MOTHER HAD BEEN WALKING SINCE EARLY MORNING. IT WAS NOW LATE AFTERNOON AND QUNU, THEIR VILLAGE, WAS FAR BEHIND THEM.

WHY ARE WE GOING TO MQHEKEZWENI, MOTHER?

NELSON MANDELA'S REAL NAME WAS ROLIHLAHLA DALIBHUNGA. IN THE LANGUAGE OF THE THEMBU TRIBE, ROLIHLAHLA MEANT "SHAKER OF TREES." IT COULD ALSO MEAN "TROUBLEMAKER." HIS TEACHER AT SCHOOL CALLED HIM "NELSON."

IT IS WHERE CHIEF JONGINTABA LIVES. BEFORE HE DIED, YOUR FATHER HELPED THE CHIEF TO BECOME GOVERNOR.

YOU ARE OF ROYAL BLOOD, AND THE CHIEF HAS AGREED TO BE YOUR GUARDIAN. MQHEKEZWENI IS TO BE YOUR NEW HOME.

MANDELA AND HIS MOTHER ARRIVED AT THE CAPITAL OF THE THEMBU TRIBE, IN THE SOUTH AFRICAN REGION OF TRANSKEI.

I HAVE NEVER SEEN ANYTHING SO GRAND!

LOOK! AN AFRICAN, WEARING WHITE MAN'S CLOTHING. HE ALSO HAS A CAR! WHO IS HE?

HE IS JONGINTABA, NELSON, YOUR GUARDIAN.

I MUST LEAVE YOU NOW. BE STRONG, MY BOY.

MANDELA QUICKLY SETTLED IN AND FOUND NEW FRIENDS, INCLUDING THE CHIEF'S ELDEST SON, JUSTICE.

SOMETIMES HE WOULD SIT AND LISTEN TO THE COUNCIL MEETINGS.

SOME OF YOUR FATHER'S COUNCILLORS ARE QUITE RUDE TO HIM, JUSTICE!

IT IS THE THEMBU WAY. EVERYONE CAN SAY WHAT THEY WANT. ONLY WHEN THEY HAVE FINISHED WILL MY FATHER SPEAK. THEN THE COUNCIL WILL DECIDE WHAT TO DO.

OVER THE NEXT FEW YEARS, MANDELA WAS EDUCATED AT LOCAL BOARDING SCHOOLS. IN 1939, HE ENTERED FORT HARE UNIVERSITY TO STUDY FOR A DEGREE.

WITH A DEGREE I COULD BECOME A GOVERNMENT CIVIL SERVANT, OR EVEN A LAWYER!

MANDELA HAD BEEN AT THE UNIVERSITY FOR TWO YEARS WHEN THE CHIEF SUMMONED HIM AND JUSTICE TO MQHEKEZWENI. THE CHIEF HAD DECIDED IT WAS TIME FOR THE TWO BOYS TO MARRY, AND HAD CHOSEN THEIR FUTURE WIVES.

THE TWO MANAGED TO ESCAPE THE TRANSKEI AND ARRIVED IN JOHANNESBURG.

WITH MY ROYAL CONNECTIONS WE WILL SOON GET GOOD JOBS AT ONE OF THE GOLD MINES. WE'RE GOING TO BE RICH!

I DON'T KNOW ABOUT YOU, NELSON, BUT I'M NOT READY FOR ARRANGED MARRIAGE JUST YET. I'M GOING TO RUN AWAY TO JOHANNESBURG. ARE YOU COMING WITH ME?

THE CHIEF HAD CONNECTIONS IN JOHANNESBURG, TOO. HE MADE IT DIFFICULT FOR MANDELA TO FIND WORK. ONE OF MANDELA'S COUSINS SUGGESTED THAT HE VISIT A BUSINESSMAN NAMED WALTER SISULU.

LET ME THINK. I KNOW A LAWYER CALLED LAZAR SIDELSKI. HE'S A GOOD MAN. HIS LAW FIRM HANDLES OUR BUSINESS'S LEGAL SIDE. LET ME SPEAK TO HIM.

IN 1941, MANDELA WAS EMPLOYED AS AN ARTICLED CLERK IN THE JOHANNESBURG LAW FIRM OF WITKIN, SIDELSKI, AND EIDELMAN. HE SHARED AN OFFICE WITH ANOTHER CLERK, GAUR RADEBE.

HOW CAN EDUCATION FREE US WHEN WE HAVE SO FEW TEACHERS AND SCHOOLS? IT'S SOLUTIONS NOT IDEAS, THAT WILL FREE US.

GAUR, MR. SIDELSKI HAS JUST TOLD ME THAT YOU ARE A DANGEROUS POLITICAL ACTIVIST. YOU ARE SOMEONE TO BE AVOIDED!

YES, I'VE HEARD THAT SPEECH, NELSON. SIDELSKI HATES POLITICS. DID HE GO ON TO SAY THAT ONLY EDUCATION CAN FREE THE AFRICAN PEOPLE?

LET ME TELL YOU ABOUT THE AFRICAN NATIONAL CONGRESS.

WHILE MANDELA WORKED AT THE LAW FIRM, HE LIVED IN ALEXANDRA, ONE OF JOHANNESBURG'S TOWNSHIPS.

MANDELA RENTED A ONE-ROOM SHACK. IT HAD NO HEATING, ELECTRICITY, OR RUNNING WATER. HE WAS ALWAYS SHORT OF MONEY BUT MADE SURE THERE WAS ENOUGH TO BUY CANDLES. HE WAS STUDYING IN THE EVENINGS TO FINISH HIS DEGREE.

MEANWHILE, RADEBE HAD STARTED TO TAKE MANDELA TO MEETINGS OF THE AFRICAN NATIONAL CONGRESS (ANC). MANDELA LEARNED MORE ABOUT THE DAILY SUFFERING OF THE AFRICAN PEOPLE.

THAT WAS OUR HOME!

YOU HAVEN'T GOT YOUR PASS BOOK? ARREST HIM!

WHITES ONLY

BY 1943, MANDELA HAD EARNED HIS DEGREE, ENROLLED IN LAW SCHOOL, AND JOINED THE ANC. HE OFTEN VISITED THE HOME OF SISULU. IT WAS A FAVORITE MEETING PLACE FOR ANC MEMBERS AND OTHER ACTIVISTS FROM ALL OVER JOHANNESBURG.

WALTER, WHO'S THAT WOMAN OVER THERE?

OH, THAT'S EVELYN MOSE, NELSON. SHE'S A NURSE FROM THE TRANSKEI. LET ME INTRODUCE YOU TO HER.

MEANWHILE, SOME OF THE YOUNGER ANC MEMBERS HAD GROWN IMPATIENT WITH THEIR LEADERS.

THEY ARE OLD AND CAUTIOUS. THEIR IDEA OF PROTEST IS TO WRITE POLITE LETTERS OF COMPLAINT TO THE GOVERNMENT.

THE FOLLOWING YEAR, THE ANC YOUTH LEAGUE WAS FORMED. ANTON LEMBEDE WAS ELECTED ITS PRESIDENT.

OUR FIRST JOB IS TO ORGANIZE MASS SUPPORT FOR THE ANC. THE FREEDOM OF AFRICANS WILL BE ACHIEVED BY AFRICANS THEMSELVES. WE MUST BECOME MORE ACTIVE.

ALSO IN 1944, MANDELA AND EVELYN WERE MARRIED. THEY WENT TO LIVE IN ORLANDO WEST, ONE OF THE JOHANNESBURG TOWNSHIPS. IN 1946, EVELYN GAVE BIRTH TO A SON, MADEBA THEMBEKILE, NICKNAMED THEMBI.

HOW'S MY LITTLE THEMBI TODAY?

NELSON, I WISH YOU COULD SPEND MORE TIME AT HOME. YOU ARE HARDLY EVER HERE.

EVELYN, YOU KNOW I'D LIKE TO BE HERE ALL THE TIME, BUT MY WORK IS IMPORTANT TO ALL OF US, ESPECIALLY THEMBI.

IN 1948, SOUTH AFRICA HELD A GENERAL ELECTION. MANDELA WAS WITH HIS FRIEND OLIVER TAMBO WHEN HE LEARNED THE RESULT.

OLIVER, THE NATIONALIST PARTY HAS WON! THE AFRIKANERS ARE IN POWER. THIS WILL BE BAD FOR US!

NOW WE WILL KNOW EXACTLY WHO OUR ENEMIES ARE AND WHERE WE STAND.

DURING THE ELECTION, THE NATIONAL PARTY HAD PROMISED TO INTRODUCE TOUGH NEW LAWS TO CONTROL THE DIFFERENT RACES OF PEOPLE.

REMEMBER WHAT WE FIGHT FOR— OUR OWN PEOPLE, OUR OWN LANGUAGE, OUR OWN LAND!

THE NEW GOVERNMENT GOT TO WORK QUICKLY. IN 1950, IT OUTLAWED COMMUNISM, THE POLITICAL BELIEF THAT EVERYTHING SHOULD BE SHARED AND NOTHING OWNED BY INDIVIDUALS.

OLIVER, THIS NEW GOVERNMENT CAN ARREST WHO IT WANTS, WHENEVER IT WANTS!

TO PROTEST AGAINST THE GOVERNMENT, THE YOUTH LEAGUE, THE YOUNG MEMBERS OF THE ANC, ORGANIZED A CAMPAIGN OF DEFIANCE. ACTIVISTS WOULD BREAK THE LAW ON PURPOSE SO THEY WOULD BE ARRESTED.

MANDELA WAS ONE OF THOSE WHO WERE ARRESTED. IN 1952, THE GOVERNMENT BANNED HIM FROM ATTENDING ANY POLITICAL MEETINGS. AFTERWARD, MANDELA AND OLIVER TAMBO OPENED A LAW OFFICE.

THE LAW FIRM GREW, AND SO DID MANDELA'S FAMILY. BY 1953, THE COUPLE HAD ANOTHER SON AND A DAUGHTER, BUT EVELYN WAS NOT HAPPY.

ARE THEY ALL HERE TO SEE US? I NEVER THOUGHT SO MANY PEOPLE WOULD BE SEEKING LEGAL ADVICE!

YOU'RE HOME LATE AGAIN? NELSON, DO YOU KNOW WHAT THEMBI ASKED ME LAST NIGHT? "WHERE DOES DADDY LIVE?" WHY DO YOU ALWAYS PUT YOUR WORK BEFORE US?

THEY ARE ALL VICTIMS OF THE NEW LAWS.

EVELYN, THERE ARE HUNDREDS OF CHILDREN OUT THERE WHO HAVE NO ONE TO HELP THEM. I CAN'T TURN MY BACK ON THEM.

BY 1955, MANDELA HAD BECOME DEPUTY PRESIDENT OF THE ANC. THE ANC AND OTHER ANTI-APARTHEID ORGANIZATIONS FORMED AN ALLIANCE CALLED THE NATIONAL CONGRESS. TOGETHER, THEY WROTE A NEW SET OF RULES CALLED THE FREEDOM CHARTER. ON JUNE 25, IT WAS PRESENTED TO THE PEOPLE AT A RALLY OUTSIDE JOHANNESBURG.

SUDDENLY, A POLICE OFFICER STRODE ONTO THE PLATFORM.

THE PEOPLE SHALL GOVERN! ALL PEOPLE SHALL HAVE EQUAL RIGHTS! THE PEOPLE SHALL SHARE IN THE COUNTRY'S WEALTH! THE LAND SHALL BE SHARED AMONG THOSE WHO WORK IT!

THIS MEETING IS OVER! I SUSPECT TREASON!*

*AN ATTEMPT TO OVERTHROW THE GOVERNMENT.

THE DOCUMENTS TAKEN AT THE NATIONAL CONGRESS RALLY WERE USED AS EVIDENCE AGAINST NELSON MANDELA AND OTHER POLITICAL ACTIVISTS. ON DECEMBER 5, 1956...

TREASON!

UNDER ARREST? WHAT FOR?

MORE THAN 150 PEOPLE HAD BEEN ARRESTED FOR TREASON. THEY SPENT SEVERAL MONTHS IN PRISON BEFORE THEY WERE GRANTED BAIL. MANDELA RETURNED TO AN EMPTY HOUSE. EVELYN HAD TAKEN THE CHILDREN AND MOVED OUT.

SHORTLY AFTER, AT THE LAW FIRM...

OLIVER, I WAS...OH, I'M SORRY. I DIDN'T KNOW YOU HAD A CLIENT.

THAT'S ALL RIGHT. LET ME INTRODUCE YOU, NELSON. THIS IS WINNIE MADIKIZELA.

MANDELA AND WINNIE FELL IN LOVE. AS SOON AS MANDELA HAD DIVORCED EVELYN, HE MARRIED WINNIE. THEY WERE TO HAVE TWO DAUGHTERS, ZENANI AND ZINDZISWA.

MEANWHILE, THE TREASON TRIAL DRAGGED ON. MUCH OF MANDELA'S TIME WAS SPENT ON THEIR DEFENSE.

IN MARCH 1960, THE PAN AFRICAN CONGRESS (PAC) ORGANIZED PROTEST DEMONSTRATIONS. THROUGHOUT SOUTH AFRICA, PASS BOOKS WERE BURNED. AT SHARPVILLE, A TOWN SOUTH OF JOHANNESBURG, SEVERAL THOUSAND PEOPLE FACED 75 ARMED POLICEMEN.

NO WARNING WAS GIVEN AND NO ORDER TO OPEN FIRE WAS MADE.

WHEN THE SHOOTING STOPPED 69 AFRICANS LAY DEAD, AND OVER 400 WERE WOUNDED. NEARLY ALL HAD BEEN SHOT IN THE BACK.

WIDESPREAD RIOTING BROKE OUT AS A RESULT OF THE MASSACRE. PRIME MINISTER VERWOERD ANNOUNCED A STATE OF EMERGENCY. IN THE EARLY HOURS OF MARCH 30, MANDELA WAS ARRESTED...

GET IN!

...ALONG WITH THE OTHER TREASON TRIAL DEFENDANTS. THE ANC AND THE PAC WERE NOW BANNED ORGANIZATIONS. FROM PRISON MANDELA AND THE OTHERS PREPARED TO DEFEND THEMSELVES.

ALTHOUGH WE FACE THE DEATH PENALTY, THE CASE AGAINST US IS WEAK.

MARCH 29, 1961, WAS THE FINAL DAY OF A TRIAL THAT HAD LASTED FOR MORE THAN FOUR YEARS.

THE ACCUSED ARE FOUND NOT GUILTY.

ALTHOUGH HE WAS FREE, MANDELA DID NOT FEEL LIKE CELEBRATING.

WE'VE WON THIS BATTLE, WALTER, BUT IT WON'T STOP THE GOVERNMENT. IT WILL ARREST US AGAIN, AND SOON.

I'VE CLOSED DOWN THE LAW FIRM. SINCE OLIVER WAS SENT ABROAD, IT'S BECOME TOO HARD TO KEEP IT GOING.

WILL YOU JOIN OLIVER, NELSON?

NO, I'LL BE MORE USEFUL HERE. I'M GOING INTO HIDING.

IN THE FOLLOWING MONTHS, MANDELA TRAVELED AROUND THE COUNTRY IN SECRET, ORGANIZING BOYCOTTS AND STRIKES. AT ANC MEETINGS, HE TRIED TO PUSH THE MOVEMENT DOWN A NEW PATH.

IN 1961, A GROUP CALLING ITSELF "THE UMKHONTO WE SIZWE," MEANING "SPEAR OF THE NATION," WAS FORMED. THE MK, AS IT BECAME KNOWN, WAS THE MILITARY WING OF THE ANC. MEANWHILE, MANDELA WAS WANTED BY THE POLICE. HE HAD TO DISGUISE HIMSELF.

THE LATEST BOYCOTTS WERE NOT A SUCCESS. NONVIOLENT PROTEST HAS FAILED US. WE MUST LOOK AT OTHER WAYS TO GET THE GOVERNMENT TO LISTEN.

HIS FAVORITE DISGUISE WAS AS A CHAUFFER.

NOW I CAN MOVE ABOUT WITHOUT ATTRACTING ATTENTION.

MANDELA TRIED TO GET FORMER SOLDIERS TO JOIN THE MK. ONE WAS JACK HODGSON, AN EXPLOSIVES EXPERT.

IT'S A SIMPLE BOMB WITH A TIMING DEVICE.

REMEMBER, WE MUST BE CAREFUL NOT TO HURT ANYONE.

THEY TESTED THE BOMB.

IT WORKS! NOW WE HAVE SOMETHING WITH WHICH TO FIGHT BACK!

MK HEADQUARTERS WAS AT LILISLIEF FARM AT RIVONIA, NEAR JOHANNESBURG.

AT THE FARM, MANDELA COULD SPEND TIME WITH WINNIE AND THEIR DAUGHTERS IN SAFETY.

IN THE EARLY HOURS OF DECEMBER 16, 1961, THE MK STRUCK. BOMBS EXPLODED AT GOVERNMENT OFFICES AND AT POWER STATIONS THROUGHOUT THE COUNTRY. TARGETS WERE CHOSEN CAREFULLY TO AVOID HARMING PEOPLE.

IN DECEMBER 1961, MANDELA FLEW OVER VICTORIA FALLS INTO THE AFRICAN COUNTRY OF TANZANIA. HE HAD BEEN SENT ABROAD BY THE ANC TO GAIN SUPPORT FROM OTHER AFRICAN COUNTRIES.

FROM TANZANIA, MANDELA FLEW TO ACCRA, IN THE AFRICAN COUNTRY OF GHANA, TO MEET HIS OLD FRIEND OLIVER TAMBO.

YOU DON'T HAVE AN EASY JOB, NELSON. THE PAC HAS BEEN BUSY.

...AND THAT WE ARE NOT CONCERNED WITH AFRICAN FREEDOM.

DON'T WORRY, OLIVER. I WILL TELL THEM THE TRUTH.

THEY ARE TELLING EVERYONE THAT THE ANC IS A POORLY RUN ORGANIZATION...

MANDELA STUDIED THE AFRICAN CULTURE OF EACH COUNTRY HE VISITED, FROM THE MONUMENTS OF EGYPT...

...TO THE MARKETS OF MOROCCO...

...TO THE HUGE MUD BUILDINGS OF MALI.

THEN MANDELA WENT TO ETHIOPIA FOR MILITARY TRAINING ALONG WITH OTHER MK FIGHTERS.

THIS COUNTRY REMINDS ME OF MY HOMELAND.

AFTER SIX MONTHS, THE MK HAD A SMALL ARMY. MANDELA WAS ITS LEADER.

"NELSON MANDELA UNDER ARREST!" SHOUTED THE NEWS HEADLINES. THE CHARGES WERE LEAVING THE COUNTRY ILLEGALLY AND INCITING WORKERS TO STRIKE. IN OCTOBER 1962, MANDELA APPEARED AT COURT IN PRETORIA.

FREE MANDELA!

HE SAW THE TRIAL AS A CHANCE TO STATE HIS VIEWS. ON THE FIRST DAY IN COURT HE WORE A KAROSS, A TRADITIONAL AFRICAN OUTFIT, INSTEAD OF A SUIT.

MANDELA WAS FOUND GUILTY. THE JUDGE SENTENCED HIM TO FIVE YEARS IN PRISON.

THE POLICE HAD CAUGHT ALL THE MK LEADERS. A FEW DAYS LATER, MANDELA JOINED THEM. THEY WERE TRIED IN A FAMOUS CASE KNOWN AS THE RIVONIA TRIAL.

WITH ALL THE EVIDENCE THE POLICE FOUND AT THE FARM, PROVING OUR INNOCENCE WILL BE IMPOSSIBLE!

WHY HAVE THEY CHARGED US WITH SABOTAGE AND NOT TREASON?

THE CHARGE DOES NOT MATTER. IF WE ARE FOUND GUILTY, THE PENALTY IS THE SAME FOR BOTH—DEATH!

THE PRISONERS TALKED ABOUT THEIR FATE THE NIGHT BEFORE THE VERDICT WAS DUE.

WE ARE ALL AGREED, THEN. IF WE ARE SENTENCED TO DEATH, WE WILL NOT APPEAL AGAINST IT.

IN 1964, THEY WERE FOUND GUILTY BUT WERE NOT GIVEN THE DEATH PENALTY. THEY WERE SENTENCED TO LIFE IN PRISON WITH HARD LABOR.

WHERE ARE WE GOING?

THE ISLAND.

ROBBEN ISLAND!

ON ROBBEN ISLAND, MANDELA AND THE OTHER POLITICAL PRISONERS SPENT THEIR DAYS BREAKING ROCKS.

QUIET THERE. NO TALKING!

EACH DAY WAS THE SAME. THEY WERE AWAKENED AT 5:30 A.M. AFTER WASHING AND BREAKFAST CAME THE ROLL CALL.

IN THE MORNINGS AND AFTERNOONS, THE MEN WORKED WITHOUT A BREAK. IF A PRISONER TOOK A REST HE WAS PUNISHED.

THEY WERE FED CORN PORRIDGE THREE TIMES A DAY. MEAT AND VEGETABLES WERE SOMETIMES ADDED.

AT 4:30 P.M. THEY WERE LOCKED IN THEIR CELLS.

THE CELLS WERE DAMP. PRISONERS HAD STRAW MATS TO SLEEP ON AND THREE THIN BLANKETS TO KEEP THEM WARM. THE LIGHTS WERE LEFT ON ALL THE TIME.

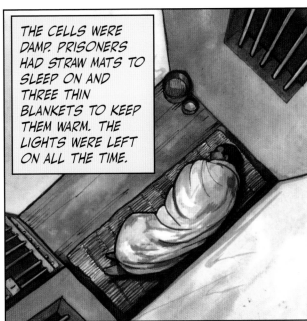

AFTER A FEW WEEKS...

LAST WEEK YOU FILLED THE ROCK CONTAINER HALF FULL WITH GRAVEL. THIS WEEK IT IS TWO THIRDS FULL. NEXT TIME YOU WILL FILL IT TO THE TOP!

WE CANNOT LET THEM DO THIS TO US. WE MUST FIGHT BACK SOMEHOW!

THE PRISONERS DECIDED TO WORK SLOWLY IN PROTEST.

WHAT'S WRONG WITH YOU ALL? COME ON! WORK FASTER!

THE GUARDS COULD DO NOTHING. IT WAS THE PRISONERS' FIRST VICTORY.

AFTER A FEW MONTHS, THE PRISONERS WERE TAKEN TO THE LIME QUARRY.

DIGGING OUT THE LIMESTONE WAS HARDER THAN BREAKING ROCKS.

YOU MEN, PUT YOUR BACKS INTO IT!

THEY DID GET AN UNEXPECTED REWARD, THOUGH—NEWS. NEWSPAPERS WERE FORBIDDEN IN THE PRISON.

THE LEFTOVER SHEETS OF NEWSPAPER THAT THE GUARDS USED TO WRAP UP THEIR LUNCHES WERE LIKE GOLD.

EACH PRISONER WAS ALLOWED TWO LETTERS A YEAR. THESE WERE OFTEN HEAVILY CENSORED.

THEY FOUND WAYS OF SMUGGLING NEWS IN AND OUT OF THE JAIL WITH THE HELP OF OTHER PRISONERS.

THEY'VE CUT OUT SO MUCH THAT IT SAYS LITTLE MORE THAN "DEAR NELSON" AND "BEST WISHES!"

IT WAS THROUGH A SMUGGLED NOTE THAT, IN 1966, THE PRISONERS IN B WING LEARNED OF A HUNGER STRIKE IN F AND G WINGS.

NELSON, WHY SHOULD WE HELP THEM? THEY ARE COMMON CRIMINALS. WE DON'T EVEN KNOW WHY THEY ARE ON HUNGER STRIKE.

IT DOESN'T MATTER. WE MUST SHOW OUR SUPPORT AND START A HUNGER STRIKE OF OUR OWN.

F AND G WINGS WANTED BETTER CONDITIONS. THE AUTHORITIES TRIED THEIR BEST TO BREAK THE STRIKE.

LATER...

HAVE YOU HEARD? THE GUARDS ARE REFUSING TO USE THEIR CAFETERIA. THEY WANT BETTER CONDITIONS, TOO. THEY THINK THAT IF WE CAN DO IT, SO CAN THEY!

FOR THE FIRST TIME, WE GET FOOD THAT'S FIT TO EAT, AND WE CAN'T TOUCH IT!

AFTER A FEW DAYS, THE AUTHORITIES GAVE IN. IT WAS ANOTHER VICTORY FOR THE PRISONERS.

PRISONERS WERE ALLOWED TWO FAMILY VISITS A YEAR. WINNIE VISITED MANDELA ON THE ISLAND FOR ONLY THE SECOND TIME IN 1966. THEY WERE ONLY ALLOWED TO TALK ABOUT FAMILY MATTERS.

TIME'S UP!

SO SOON?

IN JULY 1969, MANDELA RECEIVED A TELEGRAM.

THEMBI!

NELSON, WHAT'S WRONG?

HERE.

IT WAS A CAR ACCIDENT. HE WAS 25, WALTER. THEY WOULD NOT LET ME GO TO MY MOTHER'S FUNERAL, AND NOW THEY WILL NOT LET ME GO TO MY SON'S.

ONE DAY, THE PRISONERS WERE NOT TAKEN TO THE QUARRY.

THE SEA!

LOOK! THERE'S CAPE TOWN!

QUIET DOWN! COLLECT THE SEAWEED AND LAY IT ON THE BEACH TO DRY.

A CRAYFISH! PERFECT FOR THE POT!

COLLECTING THE SEAWEED (TO BE MADE INTO FERTILIZER) WAS NOT EASY. EVEN SO, THE MEN ENJOYED THE OPEN SPACE. THEY COULD WATCH THE SHIPS AND FISHING VESSELS SAILING PAST, AND THE ROBBEN ISLAND PENGUINS. THEY FOUND OTHER BENEFITS, AS WELL.

SEAFOOD STEW!

MEANWHILE, MANDELA HAD BECOME THE SPOKESPERSON FOR THE PRISONERS. HE VOICED THEIR DEMANDS YEAR...

...AFTER YEAR...

AN END TO MANUAL LABOR.

WHAT IS IT THIS TIME, MANDELA?

COMMANDER, WE DEMAND BETTER FOOD AND CLOTHING.

...AFTER YEAR...

...AFTER YEAR.

NEWSPAPERS.

BOOKS.

WHILE THE PRISONERS FOUGHT FOR THEIR RIGHTS, CHILDREN IN A TOWN NEARBY WERE FIGHTING FOR THEIRS. IN 1976, POLICE OPENED FIRE ON THEM. THE RIOTS THAT FOLLOWED LASTED EIGHT MONTHS. DURING THAT TIME, 575 PEOPLE WERE KILLED, A QUARTER OF THEM CHILDREN.

DOWN WITH AFRIKAANS

WE DO NOT WANT AFRIKAANS

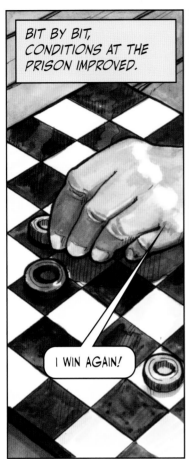

BIT BY BIT, CONDITIONS AT THE PRISON IMPROVED.

I WIN AGAIN!

BY 1978, MANUAL LABOR HAD ENDED. PRISONERS WERE ALLOWED TO STUDY AND SOME COULD EVEN RECEIVE NEWSPAPERS. CENSORED NEWS WAS READ OVER THE PRISON LOUDSPEAKER SYSTEM.

SOUTH AFRICA'S PRIME MINISTER, JOHN VORSTER, HAS RESIGNED. MR. P. W. BOTHA HAS BEEN ELECTED TO REPLACE HIM.

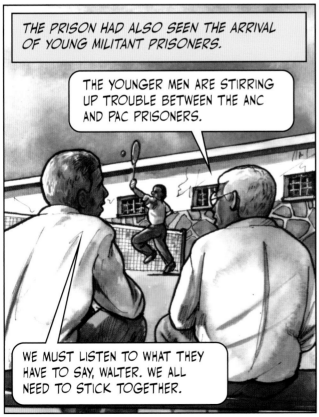

THE PRISON HAD ALSO SEEN THE ARRIVAL OF YOUNG MILITANT PRISONERS.

THE YOUNGER MEN ARE STIRRING UP TROUBLE BETWEEN THE ANC AND PAC PRISONERS.

WE MUST LISTEN TO WHAT THEY HAVE TO SAY, WALTER. WE ALL NEED TO STICK TOGETHER.

TO THESE YOUNGSTERS WE ARE SEEN AS WEAK!

WE WERE YOUNG HOTHEADS ONCE WHO THOUGHT OUR LEADERS WERE TOO WEAK. THEY WILL LEARN TO BE PATIENT.

MARCH 31, 1982...

MANDELA, PACK YOUR THINGS. YOU'RE LEAVING.

MANDELA HAD BEEN ON ROBBEN ISLAND FOR EIGHTEEN YEARS. THE NEXT SIX WERE TO BE SPENT IN POLLSMOOR PRISON ON THE MAINLAND. WITH HIM WERE SISULU, RAYMOND MHLABA, AND ANDREW MLANGENI. LATER, AHMED KATHRADA JOINED THEM.

BEDS WITH SHEETS!

AND A BATHROOM WITH TOWELS!

WHY ARE WE HERE, THOUGH?

THEY WOULD NOT HAVE MOVED US WITHOUT A REASON.

SEND THE RECORDING TO HEADQUARTERS WHEN YOU'RE DONE.

MAYBE THEY WANT TO KEEP US AWAY FROM THE YOUNGER ANC MEMBERS.

AT POLLSMOOR THEY DID NOT HAVE TO WORK. MANDELA STARTED A GARDEN ON THE PRISON ROOF.

NELSON! THEY'VE MADE A POP SONG CALLED "FREE NELSON MANDELA," AND IT IS A HIT! THE WORLD HAS NOT FORGOTTEN YOU.

AT POLLSMOOR, VISITORS WERE SEPARATED FROM PRISONERS BY A GLASS PARTITION. THEN ONE DAY THE PARTITION WAS GONE. MANDELA HAD NOT HELD HIS WIFE SINCE 1964.

MEANWHILE, BLACK TOWNSHIPS THROUGHOUT THE COUNTRY ERUPTED IN VIOLENCE. THE SECURITY FORCES REACTED BRUTALLY. THE MK STARTED TO ATTACK FARMS.

JANUARY 1985...

NELSON, COME QUICKLY! IT'S PRIME MINISTER BOTHA. HE'S OFFERING YOU YOUR FREEDOM!

IF HE WILL NOT REJECT VIOLENCE, THEN IT IS MR. MANDELA HIMSELF WHO STANDS IN THE WAY OF HIS OWN FREEDOM.

TEN DAYS LATER, ON FEBRUARY 10, MANDELA SPOKE THROUGH HIS DAUGHTER, ZINZI. IT WAS THE FIRST TIME IN OVER TWENTY YEARS THAT MANDELA'S WORDS HAD BEEN HEARD IN SOUTH AFRICA.

YOUR FREEDOM AND MINE CANNOT BE SEPARATED. I WILL RETURN.

IN NOVEMBER 1985, MANDELA SPENT A SHORT TIME IN THE HOSPITAL. TO HIS SURPRISE, HE WAS VISITED BY THE JUSTICE MINISTER, KOBIE COETSEE. ON HIS RETURN TO POLLSMOOR HE WAS MOVED TO A SEPARATE CELL.

WHY HAVE THEY SEPARATED ME FROM THE OTHERS AND WHY DID COETSEE SEE ME?

IS THE GOVERNMENT READY TO TALK? IF IT IS, IT'S JUST ME IT WANTS TO TALK TO. WALTER AND THE OTHERS WON'T LIKE IT, THOUGH.

I'LL WRITE TO COETSEE AND SUGGEST A MEETING. I'LL NOT TELL THE OTHERS FOR NOW. SOMETIMES A LEADER HAS TO LEAD ALONE.

IN JULY 1986, SECRET TALKS BETWEEN MANDELA AND THE GOVERNMENT BEGAN. THE FIRST MEETING WAS WITH COETSEE AND DR. NIEL BARNARD, HEAD OF THE SOUTH AFRICAN SECRET SERVICE.

DR. BARNARD, CAN WE TRUST MANDELA?

THE SITUATION IN THE COUNTRY IS GETTING SERIOUS. THERE MUST BE CHANGE. MANDELA IS THE ONLY PERSON WE HAVE WHOM THE ANC TRUSTS. THEY WILL LISTEN TO HIM.

MR. MANDELA!

ONE DAY...

HEY, MANDELA, DO YOU WANT TO GO FOR A DRIVE AROUND THE TOWN?

FROM THAT DAY ON MANDELA WAS REGULARLY TAKEN OUT FOR DRIVES AROUND CAPE TOWN. SOMETIMES HE WAS ALLOWED TO WALK ALONE AT LOCAL SCENIC AREAS.

WHY ARE THEY DOING THIS? MAYBE THEY ARE PREPARING ME FOR MY FREEDOM!

EVENTUALLY, MANDELA TOLD THE OTHERS WHAT HE HAD BEEN DOING.

IF IT WERE ANYONE ELSE I WOULD BE WORRIED. NELSON KNOWS WHAT HE IS DOING.

THE SECRET TALKS CONTINUED.

IN OCTOBER 1988, MANDELA CAUGHT TUBERCULOSIS AND WAS TAKEN TO THE HOSPITAL. THE MEETINGS WITH COETSEE CONTINUED, THOUGH. AFTER SIX WEEKS, MANDELA LEFT THE HOSPITAL.

MAJOR MARAIS, WHERE ARE WE GOING? THIS ISN'T THE WAY TO POLLSMOOR.

YOU'RE BEING TRANSFERRED. YOUR ILLNESS GAVE US QUITE A SCARE. IF YOU HAD DIED THE WORLD WOULD HAVE SAID WE HAD POISONED YOU!

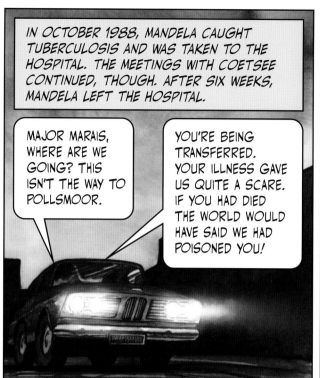

MANDELA WAS TAKEN TO THE GROUNDS OF VICTOR VERSTER PRISON.

HERE'S YOUR NEW "CELL."

IT'S A COTTAGE!

THE NEXT MORNING...

GUEST ROOMS?

A SWIMMING POOL?

MR. MANDELA, WHAT WOULD YOU LIKE FOR BREAKFAST?

I'M WARRANT OFFICER SWART, YOUR PERSONAL COOK AND HOUSEKEEPER.

WHAT?

ON JULY 5, MANDELA WAS TAKEN TO SEE PRESIDENT BOTHA.

MR. MANDELA! I'M VERY PLEASED TO MEET YOU AT LAST.

HE IS MEETING ME HALFWAY ACROSS THE ROOM. A GOOD SIGN!

THE TWO MEN CHATTED ABOUT SOUTH AFRICAN HISTORY.

...YOU CALL US REVOLUTIONARIES, BUT DIDN'T THE AFRIKANERS REBEL AGAINST THE BRITISH?

AH, THAT WAS DIFFERENT. THAT WAS A QUARREL BETWEEN BROTHERS.

OUR STRUGGLE IS ALSO A QUARREL BETWEEN BROTHERS, BROTHERS OF DIFFERENT COLORS.

A MONTH LATER BOTHA RESIGNED AND WAS SUCCEEDED BY F. W. DE KLERK. THE SECRET MEETINGS CONTINUED, AS DID THE CIVIL UNREST.

ON OCTOBER 15, 1989, THE POLLSMOOR PRISONERS WERE RELEASED. LATER, AT MANDELA'S COTTAGE...

THE GOVERNMENT IS AFRAID OF US, WALTER.

WE MUST SHOW THEM THAT IT HAS NOTHING TO FEAR.

ON FEBRUARY 2, 1990 DE KLERK ADDRESSED THE SOUTH AFRICAN PARLIAMENT.

THE BANNING ORDERS ARE TO BE LIFTED. POLITICAL PRISONERS CONVICTED OF NONVIOLENT CRIMES ARE TO BE RELEASED.

ON FEBRUARY 10, MANDELA AND DE KLERK MET EACH OTHER.

MR. MANDELA, I'M PLEASED TO TELL YOU THAT YOU ARE TO BE RELEASED.

WHEN?

TOMORROW.

THE FOLLOWING DAY AT VICTOR VERSTER PRISON...

MR. SWART, YOU HAVE TREATED ME WELL THESE PAST FEW YEARS. I HAVE ALWAYS DREAMED OF LEAVING MY PRISON. I NEVER THOUGHT I'D FEEL SORRY TO BE LEAVING MY JAILER.

JUST BEFORE FOUR O'CLOCK IN THE AFTERNOON, MANDELA LEFT THE COTTAGE FOR THE LAST TIME.

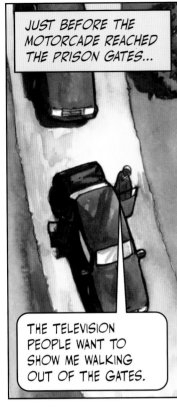

JUST BEFORE THE MOTORCADE REACHED THE PRISON GATES...

THE TELEVISION PEOPLE WANT TO SHOW ME WALKING OUT OF THE GATES.

WHAT?

I THOUGHT THERE WOULD BE SOME PEOPLE HERE...

...BUT NOT THIS MANY!

THERE WERE THOUSANDS OF PEOPLE WAITING AT THE PRISON GATES.

A LITTLE AFTER FOUR O'CLOCK ON THE AFTERNOON OF FEBRUARY 11, 1990, NELSON MANDELA WALKED OUT OF VICTOR VERSTER PRISON A FREE MAN.

THE END

A NEW NATION

Nelson Mandela was free, but other nonwhite South Africans were not. Negotiations between Mandela and the government were to continue for another four years. Not all South Africans wanted peace, however.

OPPOSITION

The Inkatha Freedom Party, formed in 1990, was a Zulu-based organization led by Chief Mangosuthu Buthelezi. He was opposed to many of the aims of the ANC party. This opposition turned to violence between the two groups, especially in a place called Natal. Many people on both sides were killed. Meanwhile, the talks between Mandela and F. W. de Klerk continued. In 1992, the last of the segregation laws was abolished.

A NEW FLAG

The new South African flag was designed to contain colors that represented all of the country's different groups.

INKATHA

Unlike other African political parties, Inkatha members were allowed to carry traditional weapons.

44

PRESIDENT MANDELA

On May 10, 1994, Nelson Mandela was sworn in as South Africa's first black president.

CRISIS POINT

The ANC had always believed that the South African police were behind many of the violent attacks on its members. On April 10, 1993, Chris Hani, a young ANC leader, was murdered by a white racist. The police had given him the gun. With the country close to civil war, Nelson Mandela appeared on television asking for calm. His appeal worked and the South African government realized it could not put off change any longer.

FREEDOM

In December 1993, Nelson Mandela and F. W. de Klerk were jointly awarded the Nobel Peace Prize. Between April 26 and April 29, 1994, South Africa gained an even greater prize: an election that was open to everyone. The ANC won. Nelson Mandela became the first president of a truly democratic South Africa.

TWO PRESIDENTS MEET

Nelson Mandela with U.S. president Bill Clinton in Mandela's old cell – March, 1998.

GLOSSARY

activist A person who takes part in actions, such as protests, to show support for a particular point of view.

apartheid A word that means "apartness" and refers to the racial division in South Africa between whites and non-whites.

articled To have trained to be a lawyer.

Bantu A langauge spoken in central and southern Africa.

Boer A South African who has descended from Dutch or Hugenot people.

boycott To refuse to deal with a system or organization in order to express disapproval or disagreement.

censor To ban something.

communism A political idea developed by Karl Marx and practiced by Lenin and Stalin in twentieth-century Russia. It states that all wealth must be shared equally by everyone in society, and that no individual may own anything.

defendant A person who is accused of a crime.

democratic When a system takes into account everyone's point of view.

hunter-gatherer An individual who finds food by hunting, fishing, and foraging, as opposed to eating cattle that has been reared specifically to be consumed, or vegetables that have been grown for food.

impatient To be unwilling to wait.

kaross The clothes worn by men from a South African tribe. They are very simple and made of animal fur or skin.

legal When something is related to the law.

lime quarry A place where limestone is dug from the ground.

limestone A type of rock that is made by the shells of dead animals, such as coral, which have been squashed together over a long period of time. It is often used in building work.

nonviolent A peaceful action, such as talking, that is used instead of war.

opposition People who are against something.

parliament A place where the government and opposition parties meet to create laws and discuss how to rule the country.

president An individual who is elected to be in charge of an organization or country.

protest To object strongly to something.

racism To judge people by their race, instead of their personality.

riot A group of three or more people together, with a shared intention, who are disturbing other people through antisocial behavior.

slum An area where many people live together in poverty and very little space. Slums are usually in cities.

township An area in South Africa that was separated from main towns for non-European people to live in.

Zulu A person from the Bantu-speaking tribe of Natal.

FOR MORE INFORMATION

ORGANIZATIONS

Apartheid Museum
Northern Parkway and Gold Reef Road
Ormonde 2001
Johannesburg
South Africa
Tel: +27 11 309 4700
Fax: +27 11 309 4726
E-mail: info@apartheidmuseum.org
Web site: http://www.apartheidmuseum.org

Nelson Mandela National Museum, Bunga Building,
Nelson Mandela Drive and Owen Street, Mthatha,
Eastern Cape Province, 5100
South Africa
Tel: +27 47 532 5110
Fax: +27 47 532 3345
E-mail: info@mandelamuseum.org.za
Web site: http://www.mandela-museum.org.za

Nelson Mandela Foundation, Nelson Mandela House
107 Central Avenue
Houghton 2041
South Africa
Tel: +27 11 728 1000
Fax: +27 11 728 1111
E-mail: nmf@nelsonmandela.org
Web site: http://www.nelsonmandela.org

FOR FURTHER READING

Mandela, Nelson. *Mandela: An Illustrated Autobiography*. New York, NY: Little, Brown, 1996.

Tames, Richard. *Nelson Mandela* (Lifetimes). London, England: Franklin Watts, 1991.

INDEX

A
activist, 11, 13, 15, 16
African National Congress
  (ANC), 3, 11, 12, 13, 16,
  19, 20, 22, 24, 35,
  36, 38, 44, 45
apartheid, 6, 7, 16
articled, 11

B
Bantu, 4, 7
Black Consciousness
  Movement, 7
Boer, 4, 5
Botha, P. W., 3, 35, 37, 41
Botswana, 4
British Light Cavalry, 5

C
Cape Town, 5, 33, 39
Coetsee, Kobie, 38, 40
communism, 14
communist party, 7

D
de Klerk, F. W., 3, 41, 42,
  44, 45
diamonds, 5

G
gold, 5, 10
Great Trek, the, 5
Group Area Act, The, 7

H
hunter-gatherers, 4

J
Johannesburg, 4, 10, 11,
  13, 14, 18, 21, 24
Jongintaba, Chief, 8, 9

K
Khoekhoen Bushmen, 4

L
Lembede, Anton, 13
Lesotho, 4

M
Malan, Dr. Daniel, 5
Mandela, Winnie, 17, 21,
  32
Marais, Major, 40
MK, the, 20, 21, 23, 24,
  27, 37
Mozambique, 4

N
Namibia, 4
National Party, the, 6, 14

P
Pan African Congress
  (PAC), the, 7, 18, 19, 35
Pass Laws, The, 6
Pretoria, 4, 25
prison,
  Pollsmoor, 36, 37,
    38, 40, 41
  Victor Verster, 40, 42, 43
protest, 6, 13, 18, 20, 29

R
racism, 6
Radebe, Gaur, 11, 12
Rivonia, 21, 27
Robben Island, 6, 27, 28,
  33, 36, 45

S
Sidelski, Lazar, 10, 11
Sisulu, Walter, 3, 10, 13,
  19, 32, 35, 36, 38, 41
slums, 7
South African Communist
  Party, 7
South African Indian
  Congress, 7

T
Tambo, Oliver, 3, 14, 15,
  17, 19, 22
Thembu, 8, 9
townships, 11, 14, 37
Transkei, 4, 8, 10, 13

V
Verwoerd, Hendrik F.,
  Prime Minister, 6, 18

Y
Youth League, 13, 15

Z
Zimbabwe, 4
Zulu, 4, 44

Web Sites
Due to the changing nature of Internet links, the Rosen Publishing Group, Inc., has developed an online list of Web sites related to the subject of this book. This site is updated regularly. Please use this link to access the list:

http://www.rosenlinks.com/grbi/nema